What Is for Sale?

R. J. MacReady

REAL LIFE readers™

Rosen Classroom™

New York

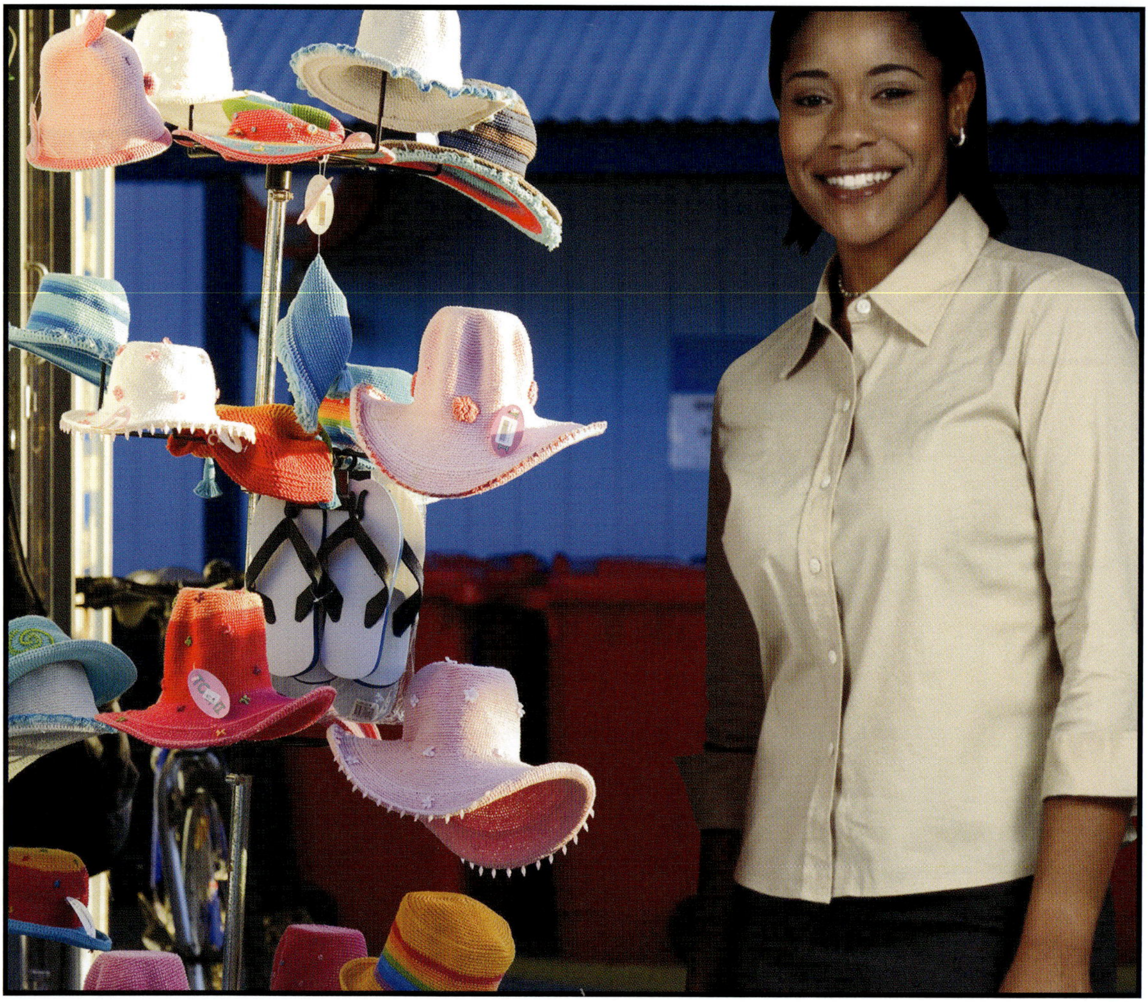

I sell hats.

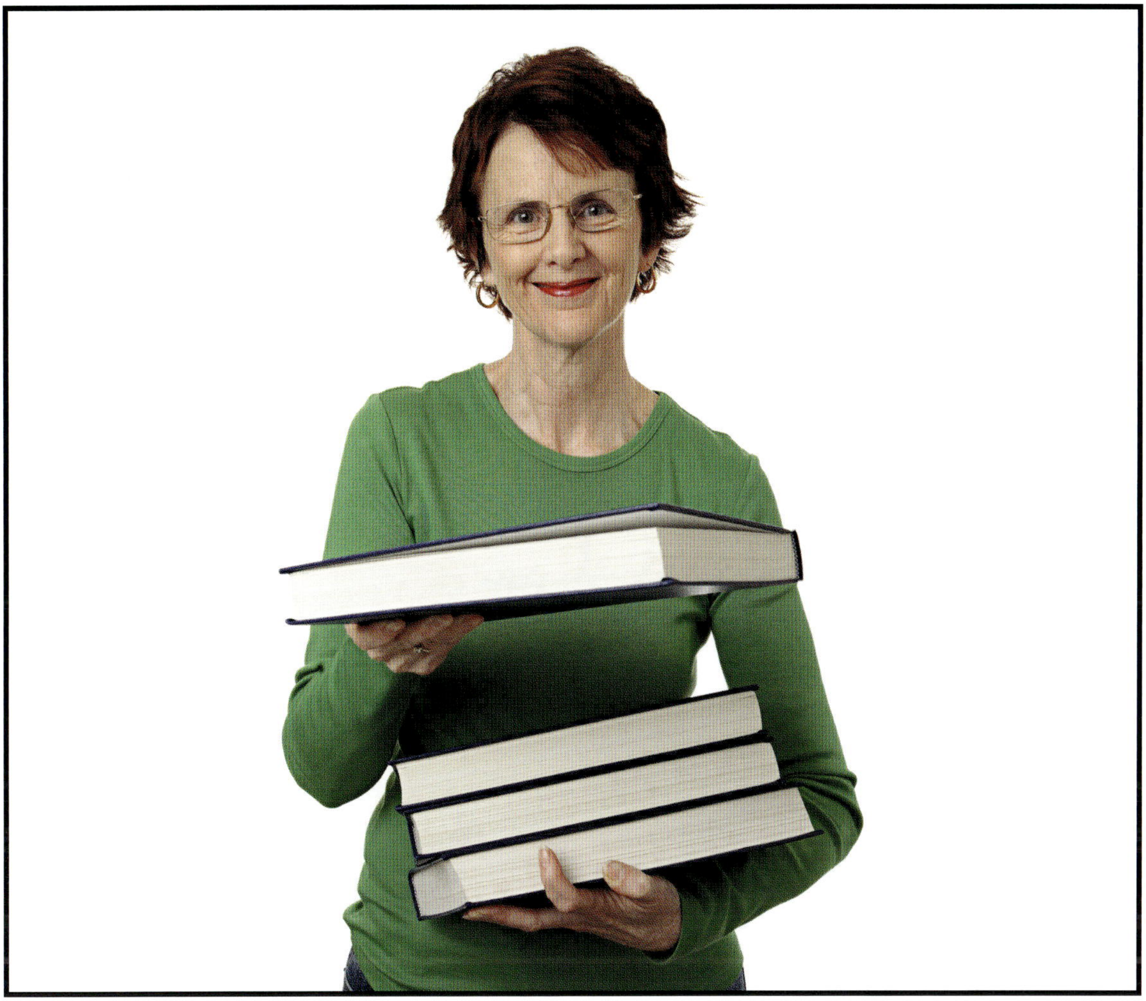

I sell books.

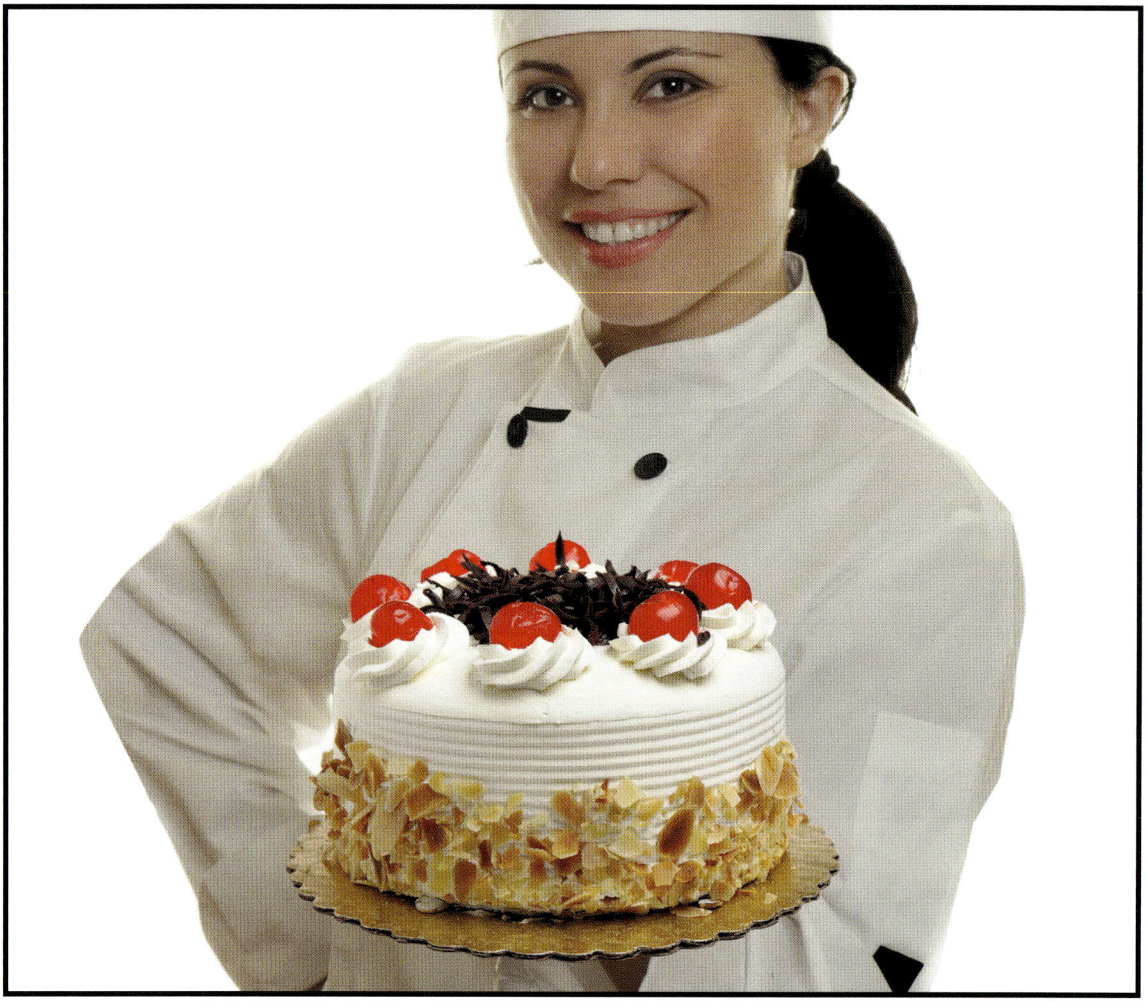

I sell cakes.

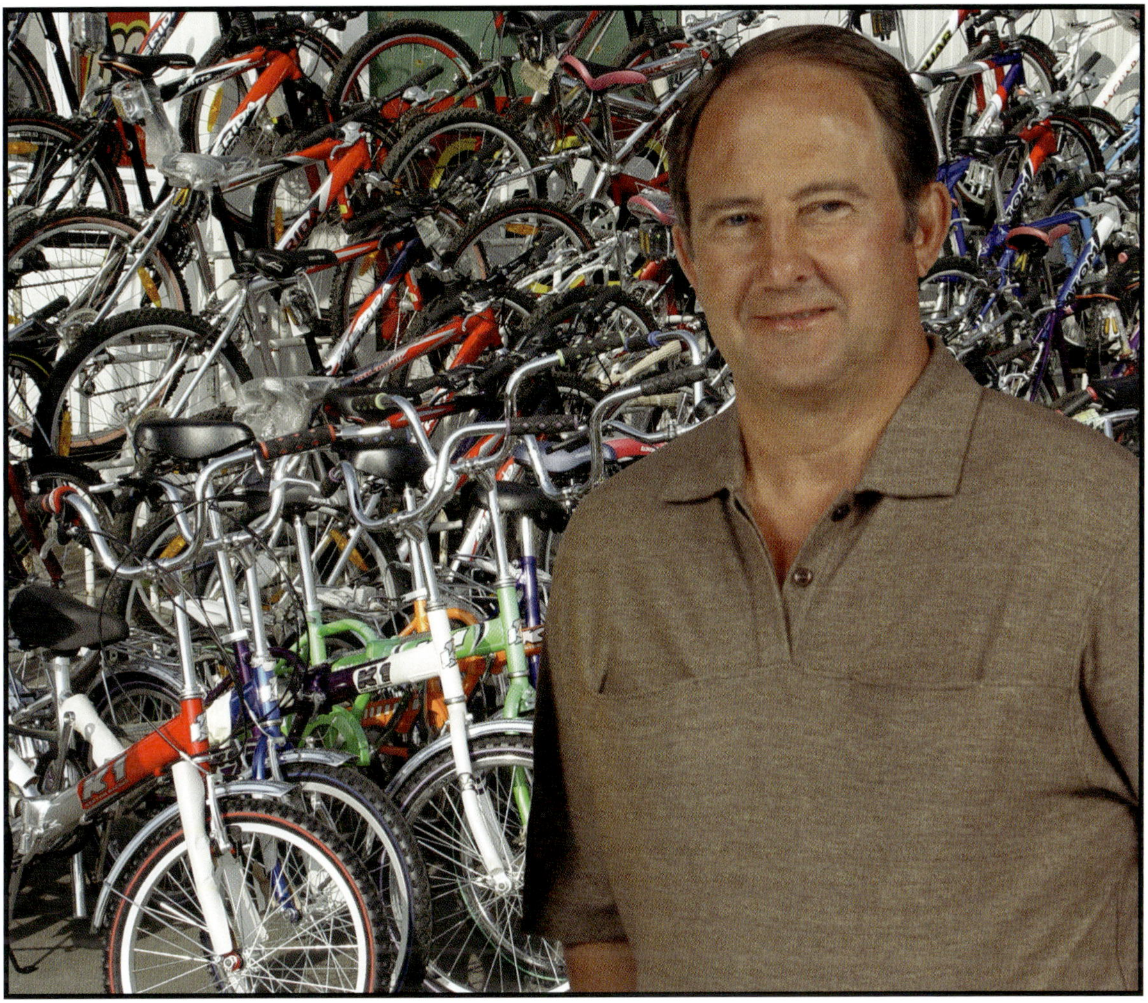

I sell bikes.

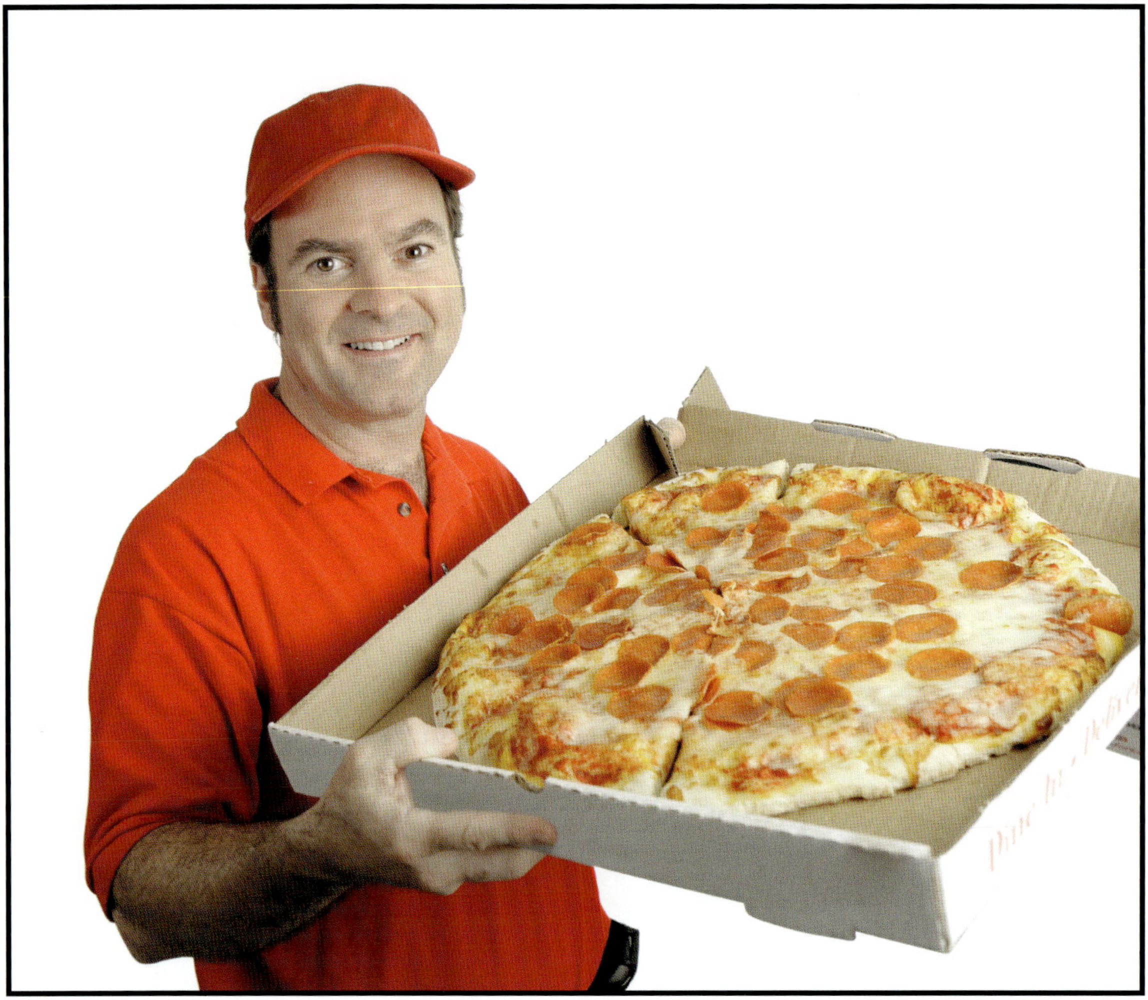

I sell pizza.

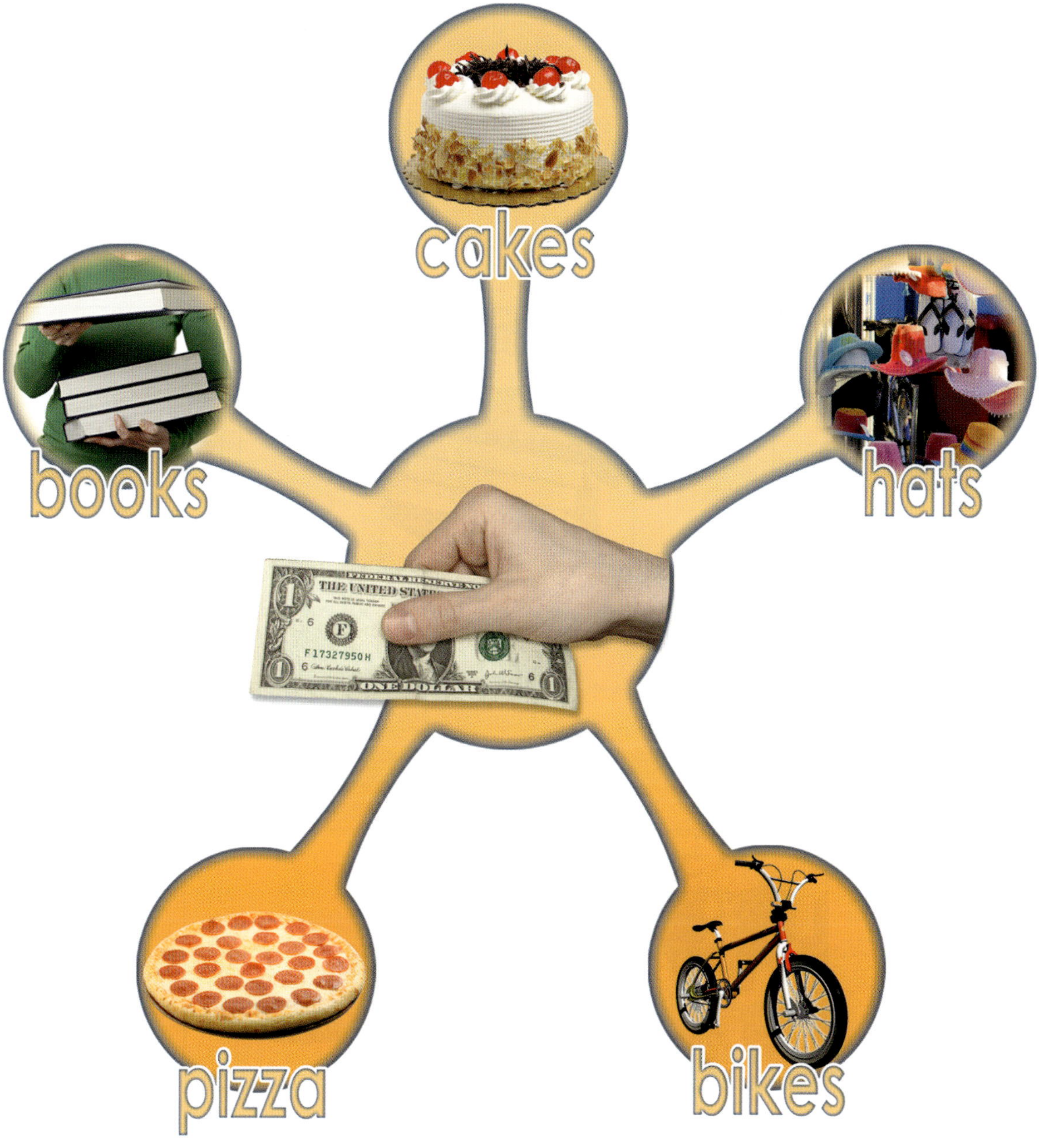

What is for sale?

Words to Know

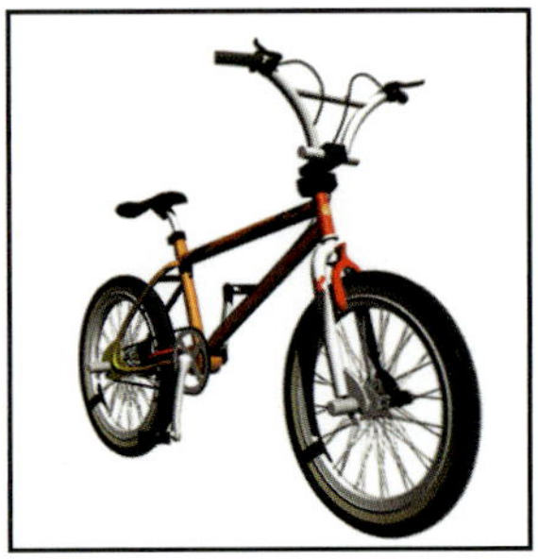

bike

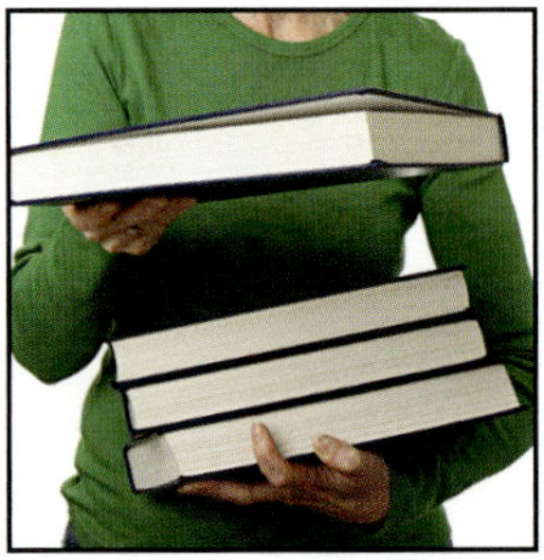

books

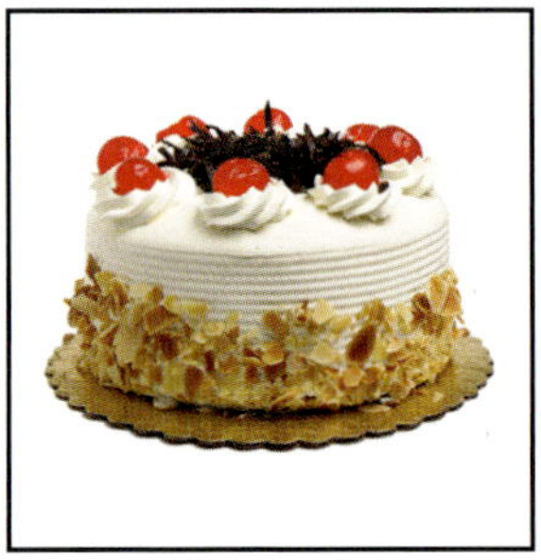

cake

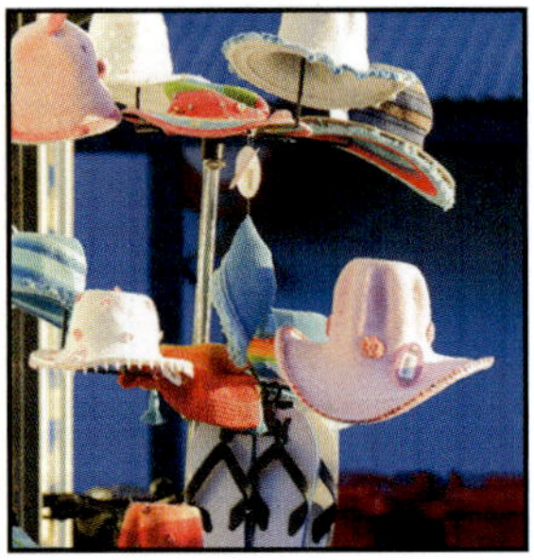

hats

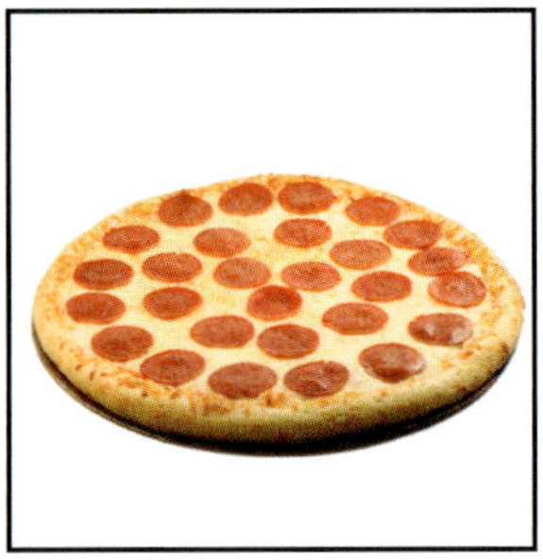

pizza